D1149375

Andy the Hero

Roderick Hunt

Illustrated by Alex Brychta

OXFORD
UNIVERSITY PRESS

OXFORD
UNIVERSITY PRESS

Great Clarendon Street, Oxford OX2 6DP

Oxford University Press is a department of the University of Oxford.
It furthers the University's objective of excellence in research, scholarship,
and education by publishing worldwide in

Oxford   New York

Auckland   Cape Town   Dar es Salaam   Hong Kong   Karachi
Kuala Lumpur   Madrid   Melbourne   Mexico City   Nairobi
New Delhi   Shanghai   Taipei   Toronto

With offices in

Argentina   Austria   Brazil   Chile   Czech Republic   France   Greece
Guatemala   Hungary   Italy   Japan   Poland   Portugal   Singapore
South Korea   Switzerland   Thailand   Turkey   Ukraine   Vietnam

Oxford is a registered trade mark of Oxford University Press
in the UK and in certain other countries

British Library Cataloguing in Publication Data

Data available

ISBN 978-0-19-919523-7

Paper use ... made fro ... conforms ...

roduct process n.

Chapter 1

How could Andy forget that day? It went through his mind again and again.

How could everything suddenly change, just like that – one minute everything normal, the next minute, danger?

Andy and his mum were enjoying
a day at the seaside. It was just an
ordinary day on an ordinary beach.

People were playing on the sand or
swimming in the sea.

Andy's mum was sitting on a rug.

Andy was exploring some rocks. He was looking in rock pools.

From where he was, Andy could see along the whole beach.

That's how he saw what happened.

Chapter 2

Andy had wanted to get to the very last rock at the farthest edge of the beach.

He could tell that the tide was going out. The seaweed was showing above the water.

Luckily Andy was not climbing over a rock.

He had bent down to look in a rock pool.

That was when it happened.

The wind came from over the car park and ripped across the beach.

It wasn't an ordinary wind. It was far worse.

It came suddenly and without warning.

Chapter 3

The whirlwind sucked things up
into the air.

It sucked up newspapers and rugs
and beach chairs and clothes.

It pelted sand and stones into people's faces.

Andy heard a flapping noise – like giant hands smacking together.

Andy gasped as he watched the whirlwind tear across the beach.

It whipped across the sea, straight towards him.

Andy shut his eyes and waited.

Chapter 4

The wind smacked against Andy's body. Then the worst was over.

But something else was happening.

The wind had blown a small plastic dinghy away from the beach.

A man was swimming as hard as he could, trying to catch up with it.

The whirlwind had gone, but a strong wind was still blowing. Now the tide was taking the dinghy out to sea.

In it were two small frightened children.

Chapter 5

Andy froze as he watched the dinghy.

The tide was taking it close to the rocks where he was standing.

Maybe . . . maybe he would be able to grab the rope.

The dinghy didn't come close
enough.

It went past only a few metres from
where Andy was standing.

He was near enough to see how
scared the children were.

Andy's heart raced. He wasn't a very good swimmer, but the dinghy was passing so close to him.

One of the children stood up.

Chapter 6

A wave hit the dinghy. The child was thrown into the water.

There was no time to think. Andy dived into the sea. He made a flat shallow dive. It took him as far as the dinghy. He grabbed it with one hand.

Then he kicked and paddled with his free hand towards the little girl in the water.

The child grabbed hold of Andy. The weight of her pulled him down. He was glad he had a firm hold of the dinghy.

'It's all right! It's all right,' he kept on saying. Then, using his knee and his free hand he managed to push the girl back into the dinghy.

Andy was aware of shouting. When he looked back he saw how fast they were being blown out to sea.

People were waving and shouting from the rocks. He could make out the words, 'Hang on!', and 'lifeboat'.

Then he realised how cold the water felt.

Chapter 7

Slowly and carefully he pulled himself into the dinghy. He did it a little at a time until finally he was lying on his stomach between the two children.

Carefully he turned himself on to his back. Then he lay like that, holding the children tightly.

'We need to keep still,' Andy told
them. He noticed they were both
shaking. 'Don't worry,' he said.
'They're sending a lifeboat to
rescue us.'

As he said this he looked back at the
shore. The tide and wind were taking
them out at quite a speed.

There was a group of people on the rocks. The rest of the people stood in a crowd on the beach. They were watching silently as the dinghy was carried away from them.

'Thank goodness for mobile phones,' thought Andy. 'At least they will have called the lifeboat quickly.'

Chapter 8

Andy asked the children their names. The little girl was called Alice and the boy, Luke.

He held them tightly. He did this mainly for warmth, but also to comfort them and keep them still.

'When's the lifeboat coming?' Alice asked.

Luke started to cry.

Andy began to sing. He sang *The Wheels on the Bus*. After a while, Alice joined in. Then he did his funny voice that sounded like Donald Duck.

Luke smiled.

'Let's sing another song ,' said Andy. 'How about *Ten Green Bottles*?'

'He doesn't know that one,' said Alice. 'But he knows *Incy Wincy Spider*.'

They all saw it at the same time. The lifeboat was coming. 'At last!' thought Andy.

Chapter 9

The lifeboat was a RIPTEC inflatable. It was an on-shore rescue craft and was fast, light and easy to launch. It had a crew of three and could be launched from a trailer.

The rescue call had gone out at 3.00 p.m. It had taken only seven minutes for the crew to arrive and launch the boat.

'Three kids in a plastic dinghy!' sighed the coxswain. 'Don't parents realize how dangerous these things are?'

She knew nothing about Andy's rescue of Alice.

The lifeboat crew spotted the dinghy quite quickly. Andy breathed a sigh of relief as the lifeboat sped towards them.

In a few minutes, the boat was close to the little dinghy. The coxswain cut the outboard. The crew were wearing special dry suits. Two of them jumped into the water to steady the tiny boat.

'We'll soon have you back safe and sound,' grinned one of them.

They wrapped Andy and the children in thermal blankets.

'You look like a turkey wrapped in foil,' said Alice.

'It's nice to be warm again,' smiled Andy.

Chapter 10

Some of Andy's friends came round to see him when he got home. 'How does it feel to be a hero?' asked Kat. She was holding a newspaper cutting about Andy's rescue of Alice.

'It was scary,' said Andy. 'I never want to go through anything like that again.'

'Didn't the parents realize how dangerous plastic boats are at the seaside?' asked Gizmo.

Andy had thought about this. 'But it wasn't their fault,' he said. 'They had the dinghy tied up, but the wind snapped the rope. It was just a freak accident. Sometimes accidents happen and nobody's to blame.'

Andy's mum smiled. 'You could say that Andy shouldn't have dived in to save Alice. But he had to do what he had to do. He had to take a risk, but he saved a child, and I'm proud of him for doing it.'